Measure It!

by Jennifer Waters

Content and Reading Adviser: Joan Stewart
Educational Consultant/Literacy Specialist
New York Public Schools

Spyglass
BOOKS

COMPASS POINT BOOKS

Minneapolis, Minnesota

Compass Point Books
3722 West 50th Street, #115
Minneapolis, MN 55410

Visit Compass Point Books on the Internet at *www.compasspointbooks.com*
or e-mail your request to *custserv@compasspointbooks.com*

Photographs ©:
Two Coyote Studios/Mary Walker Foley, cover, 4, 5, 6, 7, 8; Corbis, 9; Two Coyote Studios/Mary Walker Foley, 10, 11, 12, 13, 14, 15; Visuals Unlimited/Mark E. Gibson, 17; Two Coyote Studios/Mary Walker Foley, 18, 19, 20, 21.

Project Manager: Rebecca Weber McEwen
Editor: Alison Auch
Photo Researcher: Jennifer Waters
Photo Selectors: Rebecca Weber McEwen and Jennifer Waters
Designer: Mary Walker Foley

Library of Congress Cataloging-in-Publication Data

Waters, Jennifer.
  Measure it! / by Jennifer Waters
      p. cm. -- (Spyglass books)
Includes bibliographical references and index.
  ISBN 0-7565-0237-3
  1. Mensuration--Juvenile literature. [1. Measurement.] I. Title. II. Series.
  QC90.6 .W37 2002
  530.8--dc21
                          2001007322

Contents

Measure It All.................................4

Length 6

Height 8

Weight 10

Time 12

Speed 14

Noise 16

Measuring You..........................18

Paper Airplane Contest 20

Glossary 22

Learn More 23

Index....................................24

Measure It All

How tall is it?
How far away is it?
How much does it weigh?
People can measure just about
anything.

Sometimes,
there is
more than
one way
to measure
something.

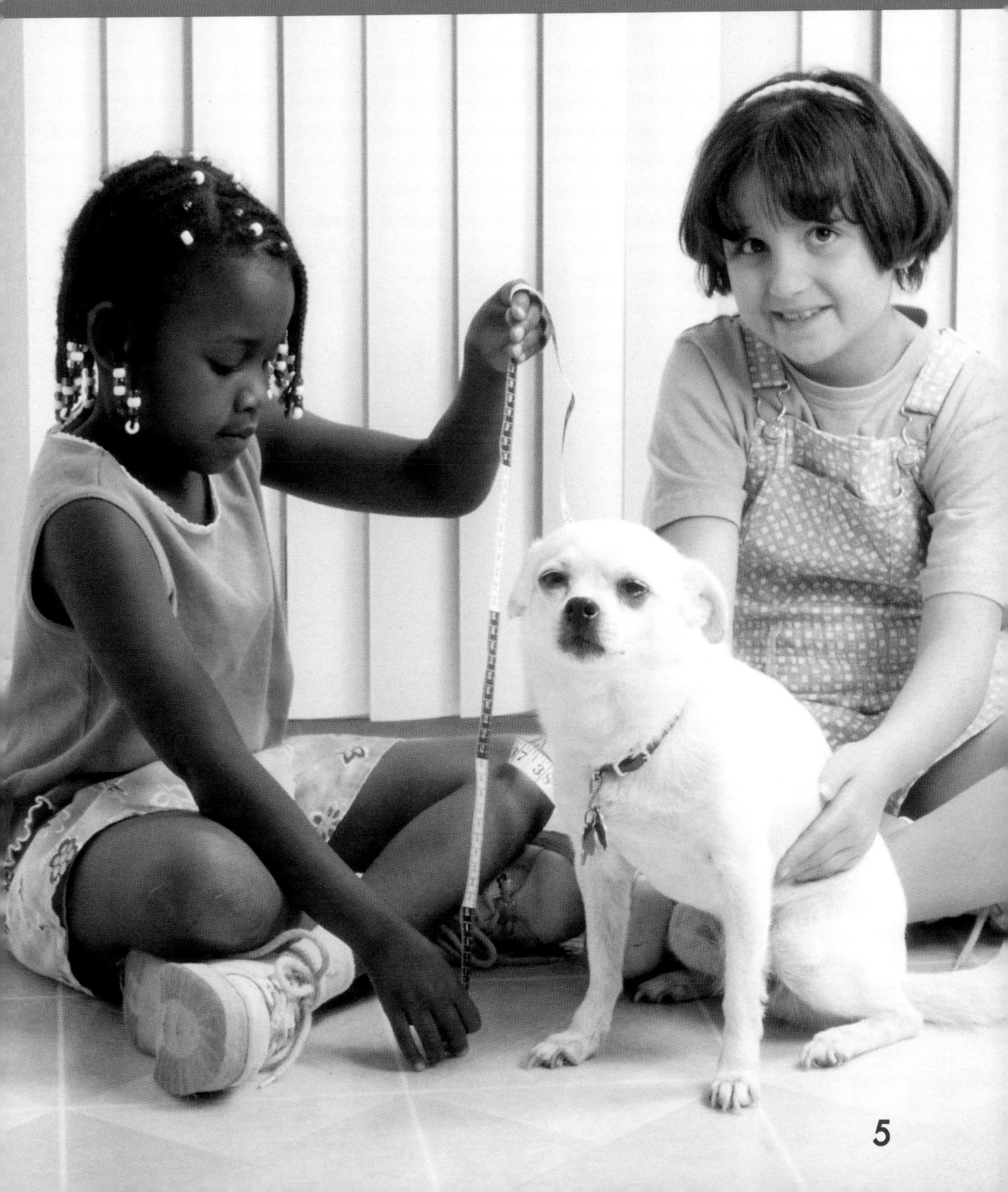

Length

If you want to measure the length of your classroom, you could use a tape measure. Because the tape can bend, it can be used to measure how big around something is.

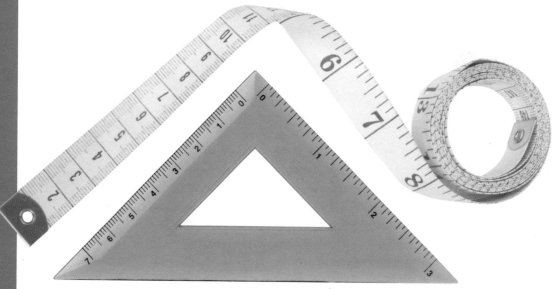

Height

Airplanes and some cars have a tool called an altimeter. This tool tells people how far they are above **sea level**. An altimeter can measure the height of a tall mountain.

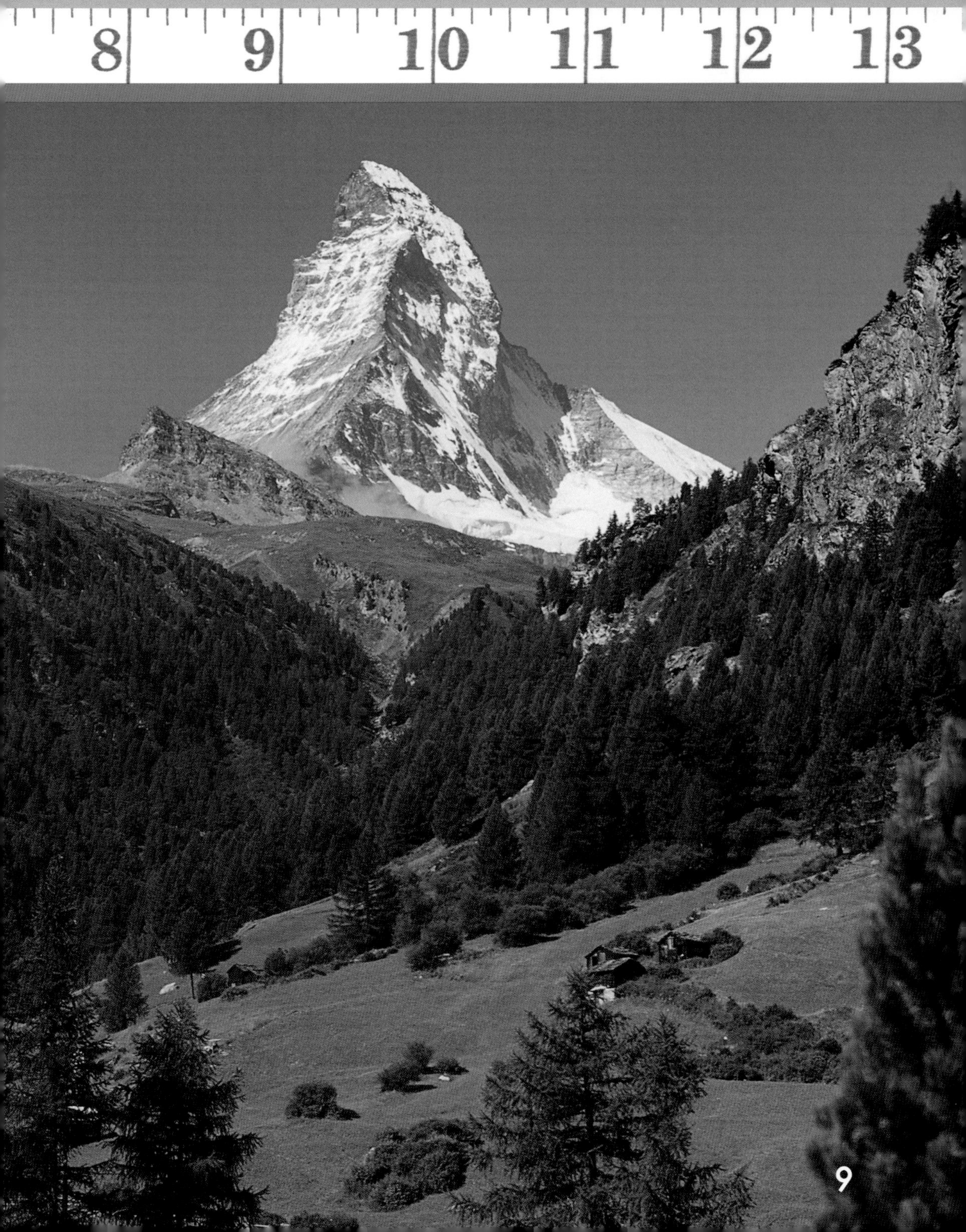
8
9
10
11
12
13

Weight

A scale is a tool used to weigh things. Some scales measure in **pounds** and **ounces**. Others measure in **grams** and **kilograms**.

Time

People use clocks and watches
to measure time.
Cooking timers measure time
by counting backward!
When a timer runs out
of time, the food is ready.

Timers

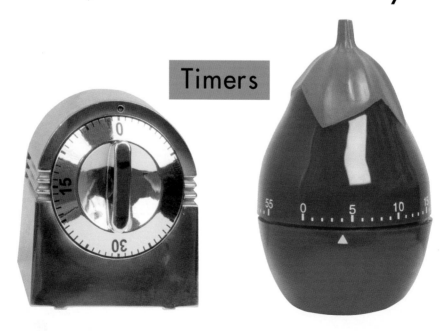

Did You Know?

A metronome makes a fast or slow tick-tock sound. This helps musicians keep the **beat** of a song.

13

Speed

A speedometer measures how fast something is moving. Cars have speedometers so that the drivers can make sure they are not driving too fast or too slow.

8 9 10 11 12 13

Did You Know?

In baseball, people point a speed gun at a ball flying toward the batter. The speed gun measures how fast the pitcher threw the ball.

Noise

Noise meters measure how loud or quiet a sound is. Some people's jobs can be very loud. If a noise meter measures too much noise around the job, workers must wear earplugs.

Did You Know?

The sounds of go-carts, firecrackers, motorcycles, or snowmobiles can damage your ears.

17

Measuring You

People get measured all the time. Doctors measure your weight and height. They use a thermometer to measure how hot your body is to see if you are sick.

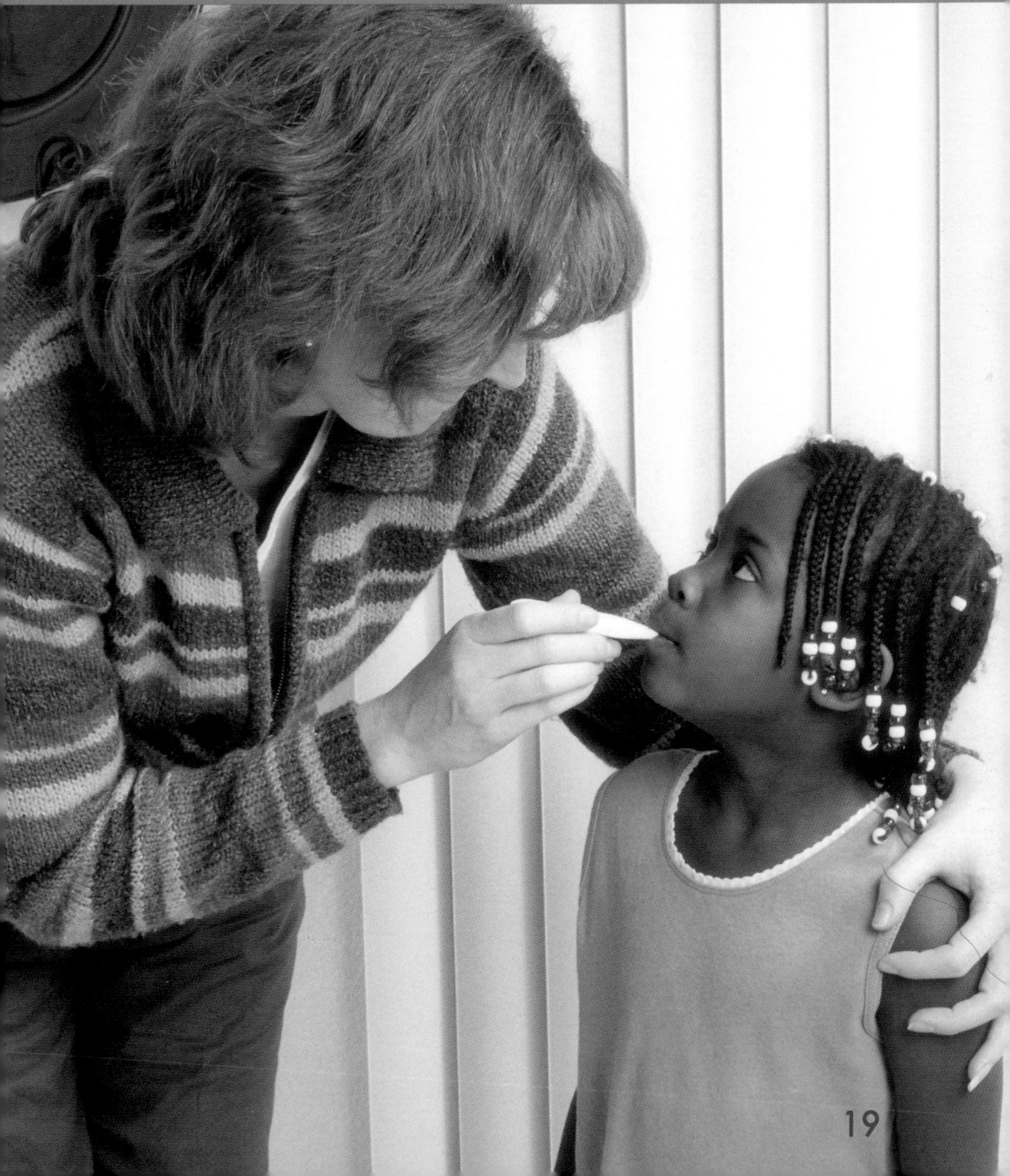

Paper Airplane Contest

1. Make paper airplanes with a friend or parent.

2. Figure out different ways to measure an airplane's flight. How would you measure height? How would you measure how far it flew?

3. In the yard, throw your airplanes.
Which flew farthest?
Which flew highest?

Glossary

beat—a steady sound, such as the tick-tock of a clock, that people use to play music notes at the right time

gram—a measurement of weight that weighs the same as one square centimeter of water

kilogram—1,000 grams

ounce—a small measurement of weight. Sixteen ounces make a pound.

pound—the most common measurement of weight used in the United States

sea level—the level of the surface of the sea

Learn More

Books

Bulloch, Ivan. *Measure*. New York: Thomas Learning, 1994.

Cato, Sheila. *Measuring*. Illustrated by Sami Sweeten. Minneapolis, Minn.: Carolrhoda, 1999.

Kirkby, David, *Measuring*. Crystal Lake, Ill.: Rigby Education, 1996.

Index

altimeter, 8

metronome, 13

noise meter, 16

scale, 10, 11

speed gun, 15

speedometer, 14

tape measure, 6, 7

thermometer, 18, 19

timer, 12

GR: I
Word Count: 229

From Jennifer Waters

I live near the Rocky Mountains.
The ocean is my favorite place.
I like to write songs and books.
I hope you enjoyed this book.

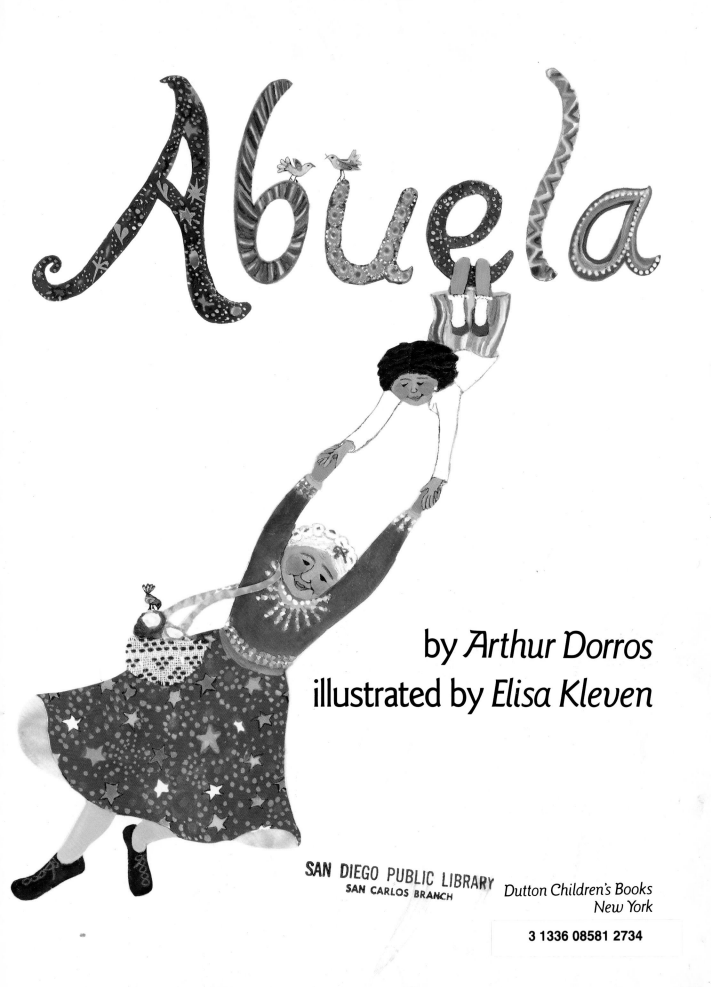

Abuela

by *Arthur Dorros*

illustrated by *Elisa Kleven*

Dutton Children's Books
New York

Text copyright © 1991 by Arthur Dorros
Illustrations copyright © 1991 by Elisa Kleven

Library of Congress Cataloging-in-Publication Data
Dorros, Arthur.
Abuela / by Arthur Dorros; illustrated by Elisa Kleven.
p.   cm.
Summary: While riding on a bus with her grandmother, a little
girl imagines that they are carried up into the sky and fly over
the sights of New York City.
ISBN 0-525-44750-4
[1. Imagination—Fiction.   2. Flight—Fiction.   3. Hispanic
Americans—Fiction.   4. Grandmothers—Fiction.   5. New York (N.Y.)—
Fiction.]   I. Kleven, Elisa, ill.   II. Title.
PZ7.D7294Ab   1991
[E]—dc20   90-21459   CIP   AC

Published in the United States by
Dutton Children's Books,
a division of Penguin Books USA Inc.

Designer: Barbara Powderly

Printed in Hong Kong by South China Printing Co.
10 9 8 7 6 5 4 3 2

The art is mixed-media collage, using watercolor,
pastels, ink, and cut paper.

To my grandmothers, *a mis abuelas*, and Alex
—A.D.

For my nephews, Sam, Joey, Jacob, Andrew,
Sean, Todd, Harry, and Scott
—E.K.

Abuela takes me on the bus.
We go all around the city.

Abuela is my grandma.
She is my mother's mother.
Abuela means "grandma" in Spanish.
Abuela speaks mostly Spanish because
that's what people spoke where she grew up,
before she came to this country.
Abuela and I are always going places.

Today we're going to the park.
"*El parque es lindo*," says Abuela.
I know what she means.
I think the park is beautiful too.

"*Tantos pájaros,*" Abuela says
as a flock of birds surrounds us.
So many birds.
They're picking up the bread we brought.

What if they picked me up,
and carried me
high above the park?
What if I could fly?
Abuela would wonder where I was.
Swooping like a bird, I'd call to her.

Then she'd see me flying.
Rosalba the bird.
"*Rosalba el pájaro,*" she'd say.
"*Ven, Abuela.* Come, Abuela," I'd say.
"*Sí, quiero volar,*" Abuela would reply
as she leaped into the sky
with her skirt flapping in the wind.

We would fly all over the city.
"*Mira*," Abuela would say, pointing.

And I'd look, as we soared
over parks and streets, dogs and people.

We'd wave to the people waiting for the bus.
"*Buenos días,*" we'd say.
"*Buenos días.* Good morning," they'd call
up to us.
We'd fly over factories and trains...

and glide close to the sea.
"*Cerca del mar*," we'd say.
We'd almost touch the tops of waves.

Abuela's skirt would be a sail.
She could race with the sailboats.
I'll bet she'd win.

We'd fly to where the ships are docked,
and watch people unload fruits
from the land where Abuela grew up.
Mangos, bananas, papayas—
those are all Spanish words.
So are rodeo, patio, and burro.
Maybe we'd see a cousin of Abuela's
hooking boxes of fruit to a crane.
We saw her cousin Daniel once,
unloading and loading the ships.

Out past the boats in the harbor
we'd see the Statue of Liberty.
"*Me gusta*," Abuela would say.
Abuela really likes her.
I do too.
We would circle around Liberty's head
and wave to the people visiting her.
That would remind Abuela of when
she first came to this country.

"*Vamos al aeropuerto,*" she'd say.
She'd take me to the airport where
the plane that first brought her landed.
"*Cuidado,*" Abuela would tell me.
We'd have to be careful
as we went for a short ride.

Then we could fly to *tío* Pablo's
and *tía* Elisa's store.
Pablo is my uncle, my *tío*,
and Elisa is my aunt, my *tía*.
They'd be surprised when we flew in,
but they'd offer us a cool *limonada*.
Flying is hot work.
"*Pero quiero volar más*,"
Abuela would say.
She wants to fly more.
I want to fly more too.

We could fly to *las nubes*, the clouds.
One looks like a cat, *un gato*.
One looks like a bear, *un oso*.
One looks like a chair, *una silla*.
"*Descansemos un momento*,"
Abuela would say.
She wants to rest a moment.
We would rest in our chair,
and Abuela would hold me in her arms,
with the whole sky
our house, *nuestra casa*.

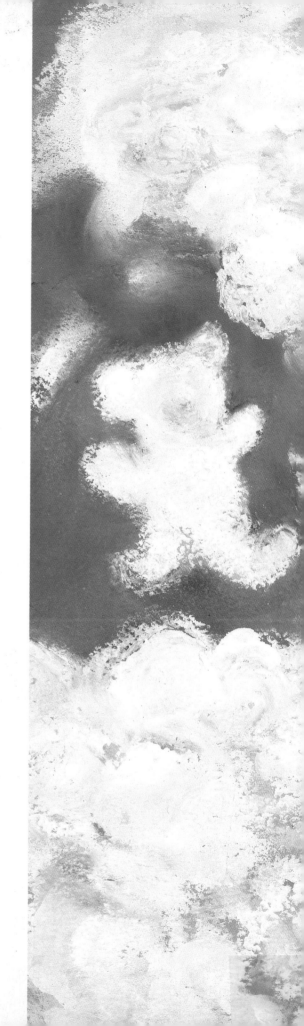

We'd be as high as airplanes,
balloons, and birds,
and higher than the tall buildings downtown.
But we'd fly there too
to look around.

We could find the building
where my father works.

"*Hola, papá,*" I'd say as I waved.
And Abuela would do a flip for fun
as we passed by the windows.

"*Mira,*" I hear Abuela say.
"Look," she's telling me.

I do look,
and we are back in the park.

We are walking by the lake.
Abuela probably wants to go for a boat ride.
"*Vamos a otra aventura,*" she says.
She wants us to go for another adventure.
That's just one of the things I love
about Abuela.
She likes adventures.

Abuela takes my hand.
"*Vamos*," she says.
"Let's go."

Glossary

Abuela (ah-BWEH-lah)   Grandmother

Buenos días (BWEH-nohs DEE-ahs)   Good day

Cerca del mar (SEHR-kah dehl mahr)   Close to the sea

Cuidado (kwee-DAH-doh)   Be careful

Descansemos un momento (dehs-kahn-SEH-mohs oon moh-MEHN-toh)
    Let's rest a moment

El parque es lindo (ehl PAHR-kay ehs LEEN-doh)
    The park is beautiful

Hola, papá (OH-lah, pah-PAH)   Hello, papa

Las nubes (lahs NOO-behs)   The clouds

Limonada (lee-moh-NAH-dah)   Lemonade

Me gusta (meh GOO-stah)   I like

Mira (MEE-rah)   Look

Nuestra casa (NWEH-strah CAH-sah)   Our house

Pero quiero volar más (PEH-roh key-EH-roh boh-LAR mahs)
    But I would like to fly more

Rosalba el pájaro (roh-SAHL-bah ehl PAH-hah-roh)
    Rosalba the bird

Sí, quiero volar (see, key-EH-roh boh-LAR)
    Yes, I want to fly

Tantos pájaros (TAHN-tohs PAH-hah-rohs)   So many birds

Tía (TEE-ah)   Aunt

Tío (TEE-oh)   Uncle

Un gato (oon GAH-toh)   A cat

Un oso (oon OH-soh)   A bear

Una silla (OON-ah SEE-yah)   A chair

Vamos (BAH-mohs)   Let's go

Vamos al aeropuerto (BAH-mohs ahl ah-ehr-oh-PWEHR-toh)
    Let's go to the airport

Vamos a otra aventura (BAH-mohs ah OH-trah ah-behn-TOO-rah)
    Let's go on another adventure

Ven (behn)   Come

The capitalized syllable is stressed in pronunciation.